D0741947

REAL REVOLUTIONARIES

THE REAL JOHN ADAMS

THE TRUTH BEHIND THE LEGEND

by Allison Lassieur

Content Consultant:
Richard Bell
Associate Professor of History
University of Maryland, College Park

COMPASS POINT BOOKS
a capstone imprint

Real Revolutionaries is published by Compass Point Books,
1710 Roe Crest Drive, North Mankato, Minnesota 56003
www.capstonepub.com

Library of Congress Cataloging-in-Publication Data is on file with the Library of Congress.
Names: Lassieur, Allison, author.
Title: The Real John Adams : The Truth Behind the Legend / Allison Lassieur.
Description: North Mankato, MN : Compass Point Books, a Capstone imprint, 2020. |
Series: Real Revolutionaries | Audience: Grade 7 to 8.
Identifiers: LCCN 2019014611 (print) | LCCN 2019016108 (ebook) |
ISBN 9780756562557 (eBook PDF) | ISBN 9780756562519 (library binding)
Subjects: LCSH: Adams, John, 1735–1826—Juvenile literature. |
Presidents—United States—Biography—Juvenile literature.
Classification: LCC E322 (ebook) | LCC E322 .L37 2020 (print) | DDC 973.4/4092 [B]—dc23
LC record available at https://lccn.loc.gov/2019014611

Editorial Credits
Mandy Robbins, editor; Sarah Bennett, designer; Eric Gohl, media researcher; Kathy McColley, production specialist

Photo Credits
Alamy: Shawshots, cover, 1; Getty Images: Stock Montage, 20, 38–39; Granger: 23, 46, 50; iStockphoto: bauhaus1000, 31; Library of Congress: 11, 17; Newscom: World History Archive, 57; North Wind Picture Archives: 7, 13, 29, 41; Shutterstock: Everett Historical, 15, 54, Joseph Sohm, 8; Wikimedia: Public Domain, 27, 33, 45, 49

Design Elements
Shutterstock

All internet sites appearing in back matter were available and accurate when this book was sent to press.

Printed and bound in the USA.
PA71

Contents

CHAPTER ONE

JOHN ADAMS'S GREATEST ACCOMPLISHMENTS

"I am not, never was, and never shall be a great man."
—John Adams

Adams didn't consider himself to be a great man. He was a complicated person. He was less charming and well spoken than other founders of the United States. He wasn't as revered as George Washington or Thomas Jefferson. But he was also brilliant, passionate, and loyal to the ideals of the new nation. His friends and colleagues respected him as a man of integrity. In private he could be warm and friendly, and he deeply loved his family. But in public he often showed a darker side. He had a quick temper. He was so single-minded that he could be unbending and difficult. He spoke and acted with passion about his beliefs, but he would dismiss any opinion other than his own. Adams didn't bother to hide his disdain for others. He made enemies easily. Even his friends often couldn't stand to be around him. He once wrote, "There are very few people in this world with whom I can bear to converse. I can treat all with decency and civility, and converse with them, when it is necessary, on points of business. But I am never happy in their company. This has made me a recluse, and will one day, make me an hermit."

Adams knew he wasn't popular. This knowledge fed his deep insecurities about his talents and abilities. He didn't think his achievements were appreciated as much as they should be. He suffered wild mood swings and depression as a result. When he was depressed, Adams would isolate himself for days or weeks. Eventually he would recover and return to his work. But this cycle of passion and depression affected him deeply. Even after he made enormous contributions to his country, he was concerned that no one would remember him.

Adams wasn't forgotten, but he certainly wasn't the most famous founding father. He didn't have the star power of George Washington or the charisma of

Thomas Jefferson. His presidency wasn't considered especially important or noteworthy. But his impact on the founding of the United States was as great as any of his contemporaries.

CONGRESSIONAL DELEGATE

John Adams was born October 19, 1735 into an upper-middle-class family in Braintree, Massachusetts. His father, John, was a church deacon who encouraged his oldest son in his studies. Adams was accepted to Harvard College at age 15. But he didn't plan to join the church as his father hoped. Even as a teenager Adams had bigger ambitions. He wanted to be a lawyer. He graduated with

The birthplace and home of John Adams was in Braintree, Massachusetts.

a law degree and set up his own law office with great confidence. Then he lost his first case. He couldn't get clients. Instead of giving up, Adams dug in. He figured out what he had done wrong. Slowly his practice grew.

By 1762, his work had paid off. He was finally doing well as an attorney. He was 26 years old and thinking of marriage. Adams fell hard for a 17-year-old girl named Abigail Smith. Two years later, they married. Over the next 10 years they had six children. Adams dabbled in politics, writing articles about the law. But he never considered himself a revolutionary. His love was the law, and that's where he intended to stay.

The world had other ideas. Adams was about to get pulled into the growing tensions between the American colonies and Great Britain. By the summer of 1774, things were at a boiling point in the colonies. The British government needed money to pay for the wars it was fighting. Beginning in 1764, its governing body, Parliament, passed a series of taxes on the colonies to raise funds. The Sugar Act taxed sugar, lumber, iron, and other goods. The Stamp Act forced colonists to pay for a special stamp on all legal documents, newspapers, and pamphlets. The British also taxed other everyday goods such as paint, glass, paper, china, and lead.

When the British put a tax on tea in 1773, protesters disguised themselves and dumped 342 crates of tea into Boston Harbor. This protest, known as the Boston Tea Party, enraged the Parliament. It passed a series of laws called the Intolerable Acts to punish the protesters. The laws forced the colonists to pay for damages. They also outlawed town meetings and forced colonists to house British troops in their own homes.

Many colonists, including Adams, were outraged. In towns throughout the colonies, people met in taverns and churches, debating what to do. Most colonists agreed that they needed a unified voice to stand up to the British. Each colony would choose representatives to this group, called the Continental Congress. Adams was surprised when the people of Massachusetts chose him as one of their four delegates.

Adams didn't want to serve as a delegate. Insecurity and doubt filled his mind. He didn't think he knew enough about the other colonies. He didn't know the other delegates, and he'd never traveled out of New England. But he was angry about the unfair new laws, so he agreed to go. In fall 1774, he joined other delegates, including his cousin Samuel Adams, George Washington, and Patrick Henry, in Philadelphia, Pennsylvania.

Once Adams made up his mind about something, nothing could shake him. From the start he let the other delegates know that he supported independence. The only way the colonies would be truly free, he argued, was with war.

The other delegates weren't ready for such a radical move. Instead, they voted to boycott British goods until the Intolerable Acts were repealed. They asked Adams

Leaders of the Continental Congress (left to right): John Adams, Gouverneur Morris, Alexander Hamilton, and Thomas Jefferson

to help write a petition to King George III, called the Declaration of Rights and Grievances. It would list their rights and their objections to the laws. Adams knew the colonies had to present a united front against Britain if they were to be taken seriously. He wrote several important passages of this document.

Adams and the delegates sent their petition to England and went home to await a response. But the king never answered them. As the months wore on, tension between the colonists and the British soldiers stationed in the colonies got worse. The king might have ignored Congress, but British officers learned that the colonists might be planning a rebellion. On April 19, 1775, British forces fired on a group of colonial troops at Lexington and Concord, Massachusetts. Right after the battle, Adams and his fellow delegates rushed to Philadelphia and met as the Second Continental Congress. As before, Adams argued for full independence. This time he had support from a few delegates, including his cousin Sam. Other delegates, however, still wanted to avoid war. Against Adams's objections, they agreed to send King George another petition asking him to keep the peace.

In the meantime, the colonies needed an army. Adams urged the congress to create an official Continental Army. He nominated George Washington as its commander. The delegates agreed, and Washington accepted the position the next day.

The delegates then sent the Olive Branch Petition, assuring the king that the colonists were loyal to England and begging him to end the hostilities peacefully. King George refused to read the petition and declared the colonies in open rebellion against Great Britain.

Members of the Continental Congress leave Independence Hall to hear the first public reading of the Declaration of Independence in 1776.

More British soldiers poured into the colonies. The Revolutionary War (1775–1783) had begun. By early summer 1776, the rest of the delegates agreed with Adams. They, too, were ready to declare independence. Together they drafted the Declaration of Independence.

During the Revolutionary War, Adams worked nonstop. In four years he served in both Continental Congresses (1774–1778), he worked on 90 different committees and was the head of 20—the most of any delegate.

THE TREATY OF PARIS

Adams had fought and argued with his fellow Americans to go to war with Britain. But making peace with the British became one of his finest achievements. With Washington's victory at the Battle of Yorktown in 1781, the United States seemed sure to win the war. Talk of peace with Great Britain began. Congress appointed Adams, John Jay, and Benjamin Franklin to negotiate a peace treaty in Paris, France.

The official peace talks began in 1782, but Adams faced problems from the start. Most of his difficulties were a result of his prickly personality. He hated the social aspects of being a diplomat. His friend Jonathan Sewall described Adams's lack of social skills. He wrote, "He can't dance, drink, game, flatter, promise, dress, . . . in short, he has none of the essential arts or ornaments which make a courtier."

It didn't help that he and Benjamin Franklin didn't like or trust each other. Adams resented Franklin's ease in social gatherings. He disapproved of the extravagant diplomatic parties Franklin enjoyed. Nevertheless, Adams put aside his dislike for Franklin, and the committee began negotiations with the British ambassadors. Before long they had a treaty that spelled out the terms ending the war. The most important point for Adams was that Great Britain recognized the new United States as a sovereign country. If Britain recognized the United States as independent, it would show the world that the war was truly over. Other countries would also recognize the United States as a country.

Adams negotiated other parts of the Treaty of Paris as well. He was able to get the new nation fishing rights in Canada. Another agreement freed all prisoners of war. Finally, the treaty kept the Mississippi River open to both U.S. and British citizens.

By spring 1784, both the United States and Great Britain had officially signed the treaty. John Jay later wrote to Benjamin Franklin about their experience, "We worked in strange but successful concert. We had in common, I think, good will and good sense. And between the three of us who did the most

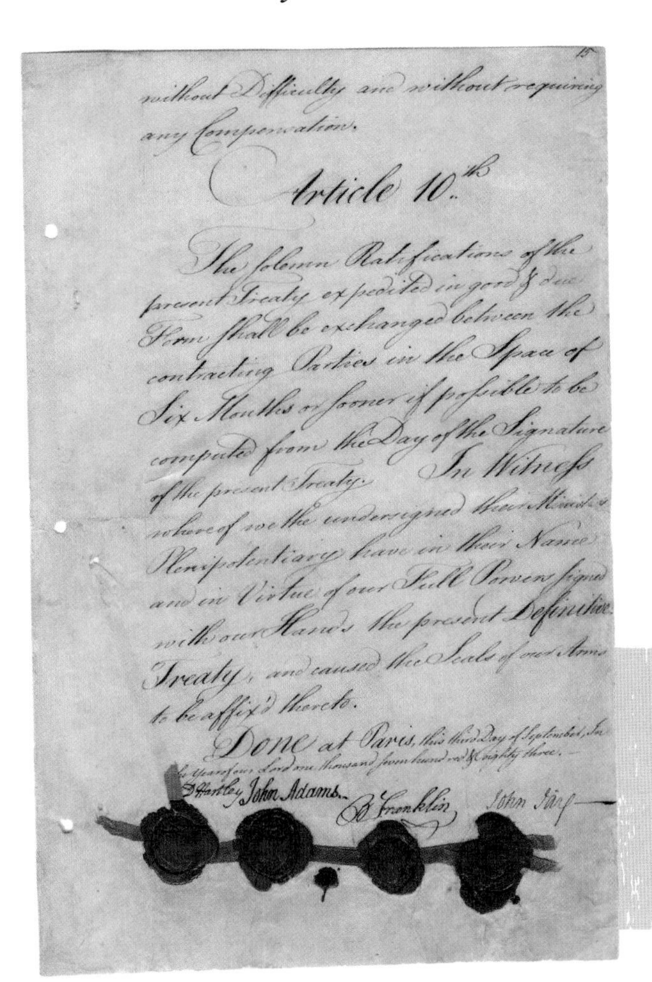
15

without Difficulty and without requiring any Compensation.

Article 10th.

The solemn Ratifications of the present Treaty expedited in good & due Form shall be exchanged between the contracting Parties in the Space of Six Months or sooner if possible to be computed from the Day of the Signature of the present Treaty. In Witness whereof we the undersigned their Ministers Plenipotentiary have in their Name and in Virtue of our Full Powers signed with our Hands the present Definitive Treaty, and caused the Seals of our Arms to be affix'd thereto.

Done at Paris, this third Day of September, In the Year of our Lord one thousand seven hundred and eighty three.

D Hartley John Adams. B Franklin John Jay

The second page of the Treaty of Paris, includes the signatures of John Adams, Benjamin Franklin, and John Jay.

work—yourself, myself, and Mr. Adams—we combined to one efficient device serving well the interest of our countryman and, I would hope, mankind."

MASSACHUSETTS CONSTITUTION

Adams served his home state of Massachusetts on the national stage, but he also made a big impact on the state itself. Massachusetts has the world's oldest constitution still in use. It was the model for the United States Constitution. It was the first constitution to create a government with separate powers and to include a Declaration of Rights. It's considered one of the greatest state constitutions in the United States. And John Adams wrote it.

At the Second Continental Congress in 1776, Adams urged each colony to create its own state government. He felt strongly that if the United States were to be independent, each state had to have its own laws.

Adams was home in Braintree in August 1779 because he had been asked to be a delegate to the Massachusetts Constitutional Convention. At the convention, the other delegates appointed Adams to write the first draft of a new constitution. Most of them agreed that he was perfect for the job. He had more experience than anyone else. But not everyone wanted him. Although they agreed he had the experience, they didn't like his arrogance. Some disliked Adams because he couldn't stand anyone weaker or less intelligent than himself. They finally agreed to let him write the new constitution, but they made him do it alone.

Adams was delighted with the assignment. It proved to him that he was respected and admired. He'd been thinking a great deal about what a new government would look like. A few years before, in April 1776, he'd anonymously published a pamphlet called "Thoughts on Government." In that pamphlet he wrote that the best government is one that makes its citizens happy. Now he took his ideas from that pamphlet and poured them into his draft of the Massachusetts Constitution.

Adams began by declaring that all citizens had rights, such as the right to

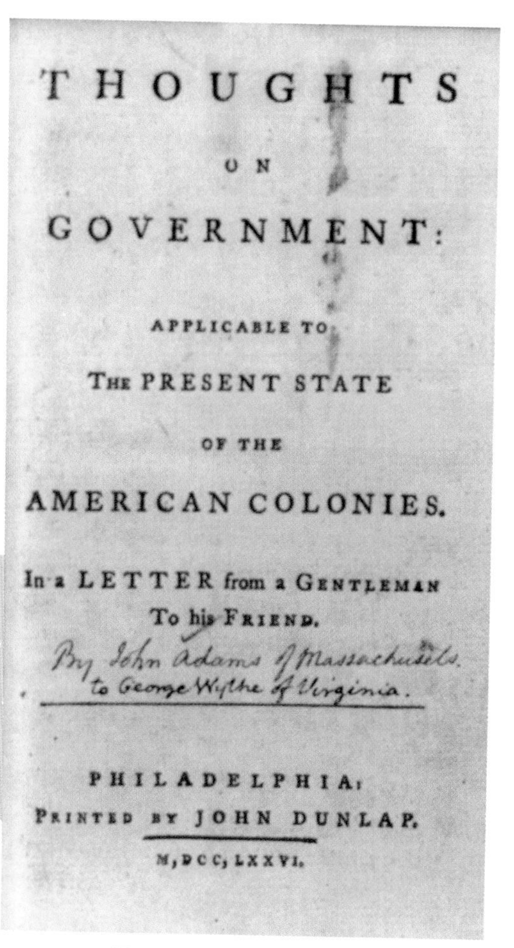
THOUGHTS

ON

GOVERNMENT:

APPLICABLE TO

THE PRESENT STATE

OF THE

AMERICAN COLONIES.

In a LETTER from a GENTLEMAN
To his FRIEND.

By John Adams of Massachusetts
to George Wythe of Virginia.

PHILADELPHIA;
PRINTED BY JOHN DUNLAP.
M,DCC,LXXVI.

In "Thoughts on Government," Adams argued for a government with three branches.

freedom of worship, freedom of the press, and trial by jury. He went on to establish a system of three branches of government—an executive, legislative, and a judicial branch. He also created two legislatures called the House of Representatives and the Senate. Laws had to be passed by both groups. This system of government would later be used as a model for the U.S. Constitution.

Adams delivered the finished draft in October 1779. His draft went through several changes at the convention, and the final version was ratified on June 15, 1780. Since then, it has been amended more than 100 times, but it remains one of Adams's greatest lasting achievements.

FIRST VICE PRESIDENT OF THE UNITED STATES

After the war ended, Adams spent several years in Europe as an ambassador to Great Britain, France, and the Netherlands. When he returned to Braintree in 1788, he was out of a job. Adams wasn't sure what to do. He thought about returning to his law practice, but he wanted to stay in politics. He'd been away for a long time, though. Adams was convinced that everyone had forgotten him. How could he run for office if no one remembered who he was? He worried about this situation during the long ocean voyage home from Europe.

When his ship sailed into Boston Harbor, cannons boomed across the water in welcome. Church bells rang out through Boston. Thousands of people crowded the dock to glimpse the famous Adams. He was overwhelmed and delighted by the greeting. They hadn't forgotten him! He realized that he could have a future in politics after all.

As Adams settled back into life at his Braintree farm, rumors flew wildly about what job in the new U.S. government Adams would take. Some thought he should run for Massachusetts governor. Others thought he would make a fine senator. But Adams wanted to be president. As much as he wanted the presidency, though, he knew he could never defeat George Washington. That left the vice presidency. His wife, Abigail, was also in favor of his running for vice president. She said that any other office would be beneath him.

Adams had a lot of support for his candidacy. But his reputation as a stubborn and opinionated man hurt him. Many wondered if Adams could handle being in second place to the great George Washington.

At the time, each state chose special electors to select a president. Each elector wrote two names on their ballots. The name with the most votes became president. The one that came in second became vice president. As Adams expected, Washington won easily. But Adams came in second, making him the first U.S. vice president.

Adams spent the next eight years as vice president feeling bored and left out. It turned out that he hated the job. He called it "the most insignificant office." Washington rarely met with him or asked for his advice. Adams spent most of his time as president of the Senate.

John Adams (in pink suit) stands behind George Washington (in black) on Washington's Inauguration Day.

He was frustrated by how little power he had as vice president. But he stuck it out because he saw himself as the heir to the presidency. The next time a president would be chosen, he thought, it would be him.

SECOND PRESIDENT OF THE UNITED STATES

When George Washington announced he wouldn't run for a third term, Adams was ready. He'd spent the last eight years in Washington's shadow, and he felt it was his turn to have the top job. Thomas Jefferson was running against him, but Adams expected to win the presidency easily. For once, Adams was confident that his accomplishments wouldn't be ignored. He knew he was known as an honest man and a respected founding father. The United States had enjoyed eight years of peace under Washington, and Adams had been a part of that. People were doing well. They could expect that the country would continue to prosper under Adams. But to his surprise, the election turned ugly.

Jefferson's supporters attacked Adams in the newspapers. They claimed that Adams loved the British monarchy and wanted to take the United States back to British rule. Adams's supporters struck back. They called Jefferson a coward for leaving the United States during the war. They also attacked him for not being a Christian.

When the electors voted, Adams defeated Jefferson to become the second president of the United States.

Jefferson was now the vice president. Adams hoped to mend fences with Jefferson, but that didn't happen. Almost from the start, the two men were at odds with each other. This hostility would last throughout Adams's presidency.

As president, Adams was almost instantly faced with the threat of war with France. The dispute was over ocean trading routes and the money the United States owed France for the war. For two years, French ships attacked and captured U.S. ships. Adams ordered the military to prepare for war. He even asked Washington to come out of retirement and be the commander-in-chief. Washington refused. Adams eventually convinced the French to make peace and stop attacking U.S. ships. Saving the United States from another war may have been Adams's greatest accomplishment as president.

When, ~~in early times~~ it was first perceived, in early times that
no middle course ~~remained~~ for America, remained between unlimited
Submission to a foreign Legislature, and a total Independence of its claims: men of reflection, were less apprehensive
of danger, from the formidable Power of fleets and Armies
they must determine to resist; than from those Contests
and dissentions, which would certainly arise, concerning
the forms of Government to be instituted, over the whole
and over the parts of this extensive Country. Relying
however, on the purity of their intentions, the Justice of their
cause, and the Integrity and Intelligence of the People
under an overruling Providence, which had so Signally pro-
tected this Country from the first, The Representatives of
this Nation, ~~containing then~~ then consisting of little more than half its present Numbers not only broke to pieces the chains which were
forging, and the Rod of Iron that was lifted up, but
frankly cutt asunder the Ties which had bound them
and launched into an ocean of Uncertainty.

The Zeal and ardour of the People, during the
revolutionary War, Supplying the Place of Government, commanded
a degree of order, sufficient at least for the temporary preservation
of Society. The Confederation, which was early felt to be necessary,
was prepared, from the models of the Batavian and Helvetic
Confederacies, the only Examples which remain with any detail
and precision, in History, and certainly the only ones, which the
People at large had ever considered. But reflecting

Adams delivered his hand-written inaugural address on March 4, 1797.

CHAPTER TWO

MYTHS AND REALITIES

Many Americans today think of Adams as a tireless, passionate supporter of American ideals of freedom. They are right. Adams was a radical. He argued for independence while others were trying to avoid war with Great Britain. He dedicated almost his entire adult life to public service and support of the new country. But not all the stories about Adams are true. He wasn't always the upstanding patriot, husband, and president he is thought of today.

MYTH: AN EARLY REBEL

As a delegate, Adams was one of the first to promote separating from Great Britain. But as a young man, his love of the law made him a hesitant rebel. From the start, he was angry about the unfair taxes the British forced the colonies to pay. He didn't like the British soldiers who seemed to be everywhere. But he argued that the British were simply misguided, not threatening. At first, he didn't support his cousin Samuel Adams and his radical organization, the Sons of Liberty. Adams trusted in the law, and he believed the British would eventually see things his way.

As the British put more pressure on the colonists, they fought back. Adams was horrified at the colonists' growing violence against British officers. Although Adams was firmly against the unfair taxes, he believed the colonists must also respect the law.

In the summer of 1765, British officials known as stamp officers opened offices in towns to enforce the hated Stamp Act. One morning an angry crowd set fire to the Boston stamp office, burning it to the ground. The mob then went to the British stamp officer's house. They broke windows, tore down the fence, and vandalized the house. The officer's family barely escaped. Later, another mob burned the house and vandalized the homes of several other British officials.

Adams was horrified at these riots. He blamed the Sons of Liberty for the violence. His cousin Samuel Adams actually encouraged him to join the Sons of Liberty. But Adams wanted nothing to do with the violence. He also thought his law practice would suffer. He decided to keep his distance from his cousin and the Sons of Liberty, at least in public. Instead, Adams wrote anonymous newspaper articles against the Stamp Act. In these writings he argued that God, not a king, gave humankind certain liberties and rights. His writings actually inspired many more colonists to support the Sons of Liberty. But Adams remained in the shadows of the growing rebellion.

On the evening of March 5, 1770, a group of citizens in Boston began harassing several British soldiers in front of the Custom House. The colonists threw snowballs, oyster shells, and garbage at the soldiers. A shot rang out. No one is sure exactly who fired it. The soldiers then fired into the crowd, killing three people and wounding two who died later. Samuel Adams and the Sons of Liberty called the incident the Boston Massacre. Mobs flooded the streets, calling for the deaths of the soldiers involved. The soldiers were arrested and charged with murder.

The next day Adams got a message from British captain Thomas Preston. He asked if Adams would represent the accused soldiers in court. No one else would defend them. Adams knew it was a risk. Everyone in Boston might turn against him. He could be putting his family in danger. But he strongly believed that every person deserved a fair trial. So he agreed.

At the trial, Adams brilliantly reminded the jury that a mob had been attacking the soldiers. According to the law, they had the right to kill in self defense. He called many witnesses who confirmed that the soldiers had been harassed first. Less than three hours later, the

Reports of the Boston Massacre spread throughout the colonies, enraging colonists and sparking the cry for war.

jury returned with its verdict. Four soldiers were found innocent, and two were convicted of manslaughter.

As Adams predicted, his victory almost destroyed his law practice. He lost half of his clients. But his reputation as a fair and honest attorney grew among the colonists and the British. For the rest of his life, Adams was proud of what he did. By agreeing to help the British, he put his principles before his safety. He felt strongly that he had showed Britain that the colonies respected the law, just as any independent nation should. It was, he said, "one of the best pieces of service I ever rendered my country."

MYTH: A GREAT POLITICIAN

One would think that Adams, who spent his life in politics, would have been good at it. Adams was an excellent writer and philosopher. He was one of the best lawyers in Massachusetts. He enjoyed a reputation for being a fierce patriot who was honest and fair. But his lack of people skills really hurt his political success. Politicians must be able to get along with many kinds of people. They have to understand how to put people at ease and listen to what they have to say. Unfortunately, Adams had none of these qualities.

His problems as a politician first appeared when he was sent to France in 1778. His job was to help Benjamin Franklin convince France to support the colonies during the war. Unknown to him, Franklin had signed an agreement before Adams had arrived. Rather than being happy about that success, Adams became angry and bitter. He thought Congress and Franklin made him look foolish and wasted his time.

His ego was bruised, but he decided to stay in France anyway. He tried to fit into the role of a diplomat. But his rude personality and disdain for others made the French

Benjamin Franklin (center) speaks to King Louis XVI of France in his court.

dislike him. Adams refused to flatter and fawn over the French nobility, which the French saw as an insult. Adams's forceful opinions and blunt speech also offended the cultured French.

Benjamin Franklin, on the other hand, loved the French. He enjoyed the parties and social outings of the French court as much as Adams hated them. Adams didn't hide his jealousy of Franklin's popularity with the French. Of Adams, Franklin wrote, "[Adams] is always an honest man, often a wise one, but sometimes and in some things, absolutely out of his senses." Later Thomas Jefferson wrote, "[Adams] hates Franklin, he hates John Jay, he hates the French, he hates the English."

Adams's lack of political skill became more apparent as vice president. In that role he made a mistake that haunted him for the rest of his political career. The Senate was trying to decide what official title to give the new president. Adams pushed for titles such as "His Most Benign Highness," or "His Majesty, the President." The senators were furious that Adams wanted to give a British royal title to a U.S. president. But Adams couldn't understand why anyone would object to such respectful titles. He refused to give up on his idea. He ignored everyone who disagreed with him and argued the issue for weeks. Finally the matter was dropped, but the damage to Adams had been done. Later, during the 1800 presidential campaign, his enemies used this mistake to call him a monarchist and enemy of the United States.

His presidential administration was also marked by political blunders. Adams kept most of Washington's cabinet members instead of choosing his own. He thought it would help the country accept him as president and smooth his transition. Adams was so sure of his own ideas that he didn't realize the cabinet would be loyal to Washington, not to him. Adams also passed the Alien and Sedition Acts, in direct contradiction to the Constitution he helped to create. These laws allowed the government to punish anyone who wrote articles against the government.

As a result of these political missteps, Adams lost his bid for re-election and was the first one-term U.S. president.

MYTH: A DEVOTED FATHER AND HUSBAND

History has remembered John Adams as a family man. He adored his family, and his marriage to Abigail Adams is considered to be one of the great American love stories. They wrote more than 1,000 touching love letters to one another over the course of their 54-year marriage.

But as much as he loved his family, he wasn't exactly the model husband and father you might expect. During the first 20 years of his marriage, he was often gone. Adams always chose work over his family. As a young lawyer, he traveled for days at a time, leaving Abigail alone with their small children.

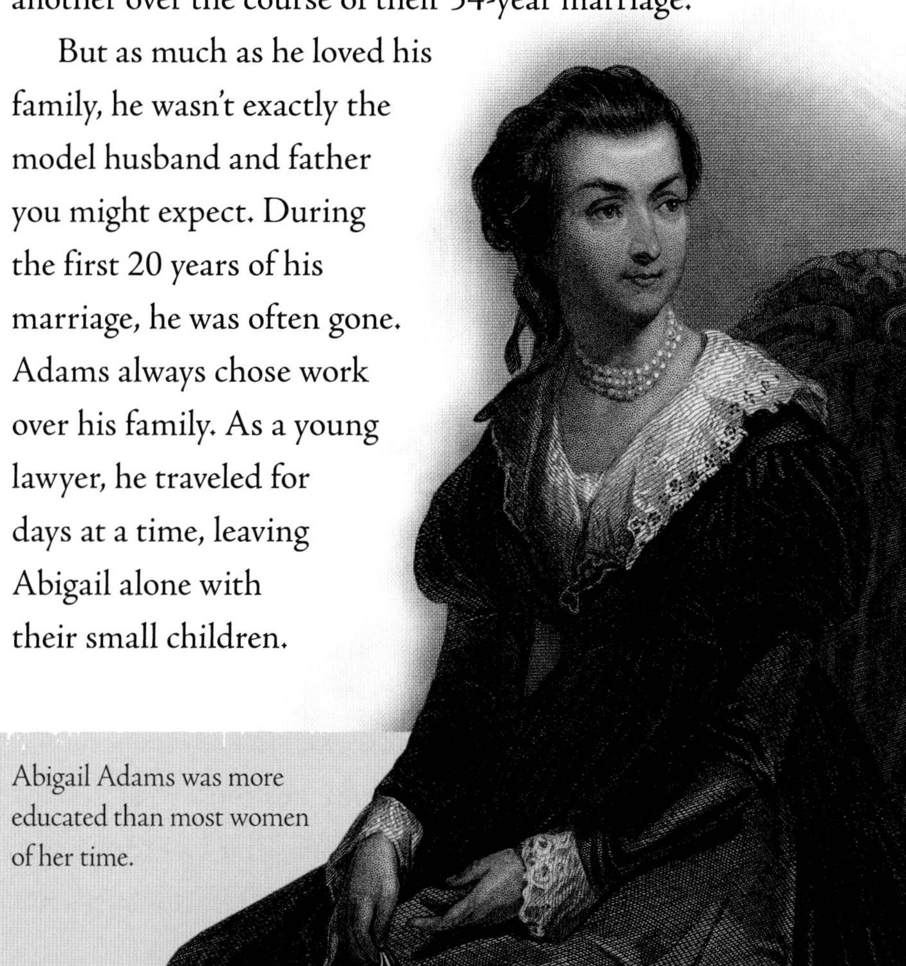

Abigail Adams was more educated than most women of her time.

When the Revolutionary War heated up, Adams's absences stretched for weeks or months. Each time he was offered a new job, he accepted it with little regard for how it would affect his wife and children.

Each time Adams left, Abigail was forced to run the household and take care of the family alone. She oversaw the farm, hired help, and took care of the finances. She was also responsible for educating the children. Abigail hated being alone with the heavy burdens, but she considered it her patriotic duty.

Not even illness or death could pry Adams away from his work. In summer 1776, a smallpox epidemic spread through Massachusetts. Abigail was terrified and wanted Adams to come home. Even though he was terribly worried, he refused to leave Philadelphia. Big things were happening. The Declaration of Independence had just been agreed on and signed. "I can do no more than wish and pray for your health," he wrote. The next year, in July 1777, a pregnant Abigail felt ill. A few days later she had a miscarriage. When Adams got the news, he was filled with grief and concern but still wouldn't leave Philadelphia.

Adams and his son John Quincy sailed for France in 1778, leaving Abigail and the other children alone for the next five years. Abigail called this time her widowhood. At one point Adams all but stopped writing letters. He claimed his work was so important that he didn't have time to write as often. Finally, in 1784, Abigail joined

Adams in France. They would be together for the rest of their lives.

Adams was also a very strict and controlling father. He criticized his sons and corrected their letters when they made mistakes. He insisted that his sons be great men someday. He once scolded John Quincy, writing, "If you do not rise to the head not only of your profession but of your country it will be owing to your own laziness, slovenliness, and obstinacy."

John Quincy Adams was the eldest son of John and Abigail Adams.

This pressure took a toll on his children. His eldest son, John Quincy, did go on to become president. But his other two sons, Charles and Thomas, never achieved the same success. Charles was expelled from Harvard and died of alcoholism after years of bad financial decisions. Thomas, the youngest, barely knew his father growing up. He reluctantly became an attorney because his family expected it. He was a half-hearted lawyer, and he struggled with depression and alcoholism for the rest of his life. He eventually gave up working and moved to the family farm to care for his aging father.

MYTH: A SILENT VOICE AGAINST SLAVERY

In Adams's day, slavery was a part of life in the colonies. Most enslaved people lived in the southern colonies and worked on large farms known as plantations. In the north, enslaved people worked mostly in cities as domestic servants, dockworkers, artists, and craftspeople. It wasn't uncommon for a slave owner to hire out his slaves to someone else. Then the owner would take the money the enslaved person earned.

Adams was quite familiar with the practice of hiring out enslaved people. But he didn't believe in slavery and never owned slaves. He always hired freemen, both as house servants and farmhands, even though it would have been less expensive for him to buy slaves. He was proud of the fact that he didn't own slaves. He pointed to that as proof of his good character and his opposition to slavery.

But if slavery was so terrible to him, why didn't he do more? He was certainly in a position to do so.

Adams, like many others, believed that slavery would end on its own. During Adams's time, slavery was on the decline, at least in the north. By the end of the war, many states had either abolished slavery, suspended it, or were moving to gradually end it. To him, slavery wasn't that big of a problem in the new country.

At times Adams struggled with the slavery question. It hung like a "cloud over my imagination," he wrote. He called it a "gangrene" that had to be stopped or there would be violence. But he refused to do anything to end slavery.

Adams felt caught in the middle. He knew that if he spoke out, he would anger people in the southern, slaveholding states. He also believed that those who did want to abolish slavery were dangerous radicals. Adams feared that if slavery ended too quickly, there would be violence. In his mind, anything that disrupted peaceful society was bad. So, to Adams, any violence against white slave owners was more dangerous to the country than the horrors of people being used as property. There was no escaping the violence, however, as the Civil War (1861–1865) would eventually prove.

CHAPTER THREE

THE UNKNOWN ADAMS

Adams isn't one of the best-known founding fathers or presidents. Throughout his life, he was overshadowed by the more powerful and engaging personalities of Franklin, Washington, and Jefferson. Several of his greatest achievements aren't well known, but they had a lasting impact on the nation.

FATHER OF THE NAVY

If there was one thing the U.S. colonists feared more than the British army, it was the British Navy. At the start of the Revolutionary War, Britain had one of the world's largest and strongest naval forces. Despite that, the Continental Congress didn't consider starting a navy when they created the Continental Army. But when rumors spread in the fall of 1775 that a huge British navy force was on its way to the colonies, suddenly a Continental navy seemed like a very good idea.

For about two weeks the Continental Congress debated the idea. Adams was one of its strongest supporters. Others, however, were just as strongly against the idea. At that point many members of Congress still hoped to avoid war. They believed a Continental navy would antagonize Great Britain. Others thought that building a navy from scratch was too expensive. Individual states already had their own ships, they argued. Let them protect the coastlines.

Adams was having none of that. He said that a Continental navy would distress the enemy. It would also protect the coastlines and the colonists who lived there. Finally his arguments convinced the congressmen. They voted to remodel two sailing ships into warships. Once the ships were fully armed, their mission was to stop British ships from bringing weapons and supplies to the colonies.

At first the Continental Navy wasn't the powerhouse that Adams had hoped, but it did contribute to the war. Colonial ships stopped nearly 200 British vessels and took their supplies. They brought much-needed weapons and supplies from Europe.

After the war was over, Congress saw no more need for a naval force. The ships were retired. The new United States had no navy until 1794.

It wasn't the threat of war that forced Congress to rethink the idea of a national navy. It was pirates, who were mercilessly attacking U.S. merchant ships in the Mediterranean Sea. By this time Adams was vice president. He wholeheartedly supported reviving the navy. Congress agreed, and six new ships were built.

By the time Adams became president in 1796 tensions between the United States and France had grown. The idea of a strong federal navy gained more support. Adams knew it was time to create a naval department. In 1798, he signed the law that created the U.S. Navy. His idea for a strong national navy had finally come true.

A U.S. Navy ship exchanges fire with an enemy ship around 1815.

CONTRIBUTING TO THE DECLARATION OF INDEPENDENCE

It's commonly thought that Thomas Jefferson was the sole writer of the Declaration of Independence. History has painted a picture of Jefferson, alone, bent over a desk far into the night. Jefferson was the main author of the declaration, but he definitely had help from a group of men that included Adams.

Adams, Jefferson, Benjamin Franklin, Roger Sherman, and Robert Livingston formed a committee to write the document. They were known as the Committee of Five. According to Adams, Jefferson actually urged him to write the document. Adams refused. When Jefferson asked why, Adams responded, "Reason first: you are a Virginian and a Virginian ought to appear at the head of this business. Reason second: I am obnoxious, suspected, and unpopular. You are very much otherwise. Reason third: you can write ten times better than I can."

Jefferson finally agreed. He quickly wrote a draft that he gave to the committee members. As Adams read the rough draft, he was delighted with the soaring language. He approved of a section in which Jefferson denounced slavery, although Adams knew the southern delegates would never pass it.

There were some small sections of the Declaration that Adams didn't exactly agree with. He wouldn't have called the British king a tyrant, for instance. He thought it sounded too much like the colonists were scolding the king. Adams felt that the document should be more

The Committee of Five (left to right): Benjamin Franklin, Thomas Jefferson, John Adams, Robert Livingston, and Roger Sherman

respectful and serious. But he didn't think it was worth taking out. The others agreed.

After Jefferson wrote the first draft, he sent it to Franklin and Adams to look at. He wrote, "before I reported it to the committee I communicated it separately to Dr. Franklin and Mr. Adams requesting their corrections . . . I then wrote a fair copy, reported it to the committee, and from them, unaltered to the Congress."

Adams and the other committee members continued to offer advice and suggestions as Jefferson wrote several drafts. There isn't much information about each person's specific contribution to the declaration. The committee didn't keep notes during their meetings. Years later, Adams wrote in his autobiography that he couldn't remember exactly what he had contributed. Seventeen days later, the Declaration of Independence went to the full Congress for approval. Representatives suggested additional changes and voted to delete the section on slavery, just as Adams had predicted. On July 2, 1776, the colonies voted in favor of independence.

Adams was moved by the vote. He thought this moment would be celebrated for all time. He wrote Abigail, saying that July 2 "will be the most memorable epocha in the history of America." He imagined festivals with parades, games, shows, and sports. What Adams didn't know at the time was that July 4 would be the day to live in history. That was the day Congress officially adopted the Declaration of Independence.

FIRST U.S. AMBASSADOR

Before and during the Revolutionary War, the colonies sent several envoys to Europe. These men weren't official ambassadors because the United States wasn't yet a country. The envoys' job was to convince other countries to help them win the war. It's well known that Adams served as one of these envoys to France. What isn't typically known is that he became the first official ambassador to represent the United States. This was an extraordinary achievement for Adams and for the new United States. Even more surprising is that he became a star diplomat.

When Congress appointed Adams as envoy to France in 1778, he thought he would be doing some of the most important work of his career. Instead, he found himself in Benjamin Franklin's shadow, as Franklin was more popular with the French. Eventually the French ambassador announced he would only work with Franklin. Congress stripped Adams of his duties, and he returned home in disgrace. He was certain that his career as a diplomat was over.

Three months later Congress appointed Adams ambassador to Great Britain, much to his shock. His job was to help negotiate peace with the British whenever the war was over. So off he sailed back to Europe.

Adams was too impatient to sit around and wait for Great Britain to agree to peace. He decided to take action. He sailed to the Netherlands. His goal was to quietly get as much money from the Dutch as he could. He was looking for loans for the United States.

At first, Dutch officials wouldn't meet with him. The government hadn't yet recognized the United States as an independent nation. Dutch officials didn't want to help the new nation until they knew who would win the war. Adams managed to put aside his distaste for social gatherings and made friends with wealthy Dutch bankers. He went to parties with members of Dutch society. But no one would officially agree to help.

Then in October 1781, the Continental Army won a huge victory over the British at Yorktown. Adams was thrilled. Suddenly his wealthy Dutch friends were more interested in talking to him. Just six months after Yorktown, in April 1782, the Dutch government officially recognized the United States as an independent country. Adams went from an unofficial envoy to the first official foreign ambassador for the United States.

Now that Adams, and the United States, were official, the Dutch government agreed to loan the United States 5 million guilders ($2 million). Adams wrote to Abigail that, "if this had been the only action in my life, it would have been well spent."

Adams's diplomatic career wasn't over yet. Soon after the Treaty of Paris was signed, Franklin retired and went home to the United States. Adams was named the first United States minister to Great Britain. His job was to mend fences and establish trade with the former enemy.

The patriots' victory at Yorktown had resoundingly positive consequences for Adams's diplomatic work.

One of his first acts as ambassador was a face-to-face meeting with King George III. Adams knew it would be awkward at best, so he memorized a complimentary speech. He also learned the proper etiquette on bowing to the king. The meeting went much better than Adams anticipated. The king listened politely to his remarks, and then said what Adams hoped to hear. He said that Great Britain would "meet the friendship of the United States as an independent power."

Ambassador John Adams (center) greets King George III of Great Britain (right).

CHAPTER FOUR

DIFFICULT TRUTHS

Adams is generally known as a man of honesty and integrity. But he could also be angry, vindictive, and downright nasty. As president, he trusted no one except his wife, Abigail. He had strong principles, but he didn't understand how to use politics to get what he wanted. Many times his unbending belief in his own ideals blinded him to political realities.

THE DIRTIEST U.S. CAMPAIGN IN HISTORY

After four years as president, Adams approached the election of 1800 with uneasiness. His administration had been plagued with problems. The war between Great Britain and France had consumed his presidency. He had managed to avoid a war with France, but it had come at a price. Throughout his presidency, the debate over the situation in France had bitterly divided the legislature down the middle. At the time the two main political parties were the Federalist Party and the Democratic-Republicans. Adams was a Federalist. Anti-French feelings ran high through the Federalist Party. A radical faction led by Alexander Hamilton wanted to go to war as retaliation for the French attacks on U.S. ships. They opposed Adams's efforts to maintain peace. On the other side, Jefferson and the pro-French Democratic-Republicans grew alarmed and angry. By 1800, the two parties were openly fighting. At one point, two congressmen, Federalist Roger Griswold and Democratic-Republican Matthew Lyon, got into a brawl in the House. They attacked each other with canes and fire tongs before others broke up the fight. Tensions were high as the presidential campaign of 1800 began.

Adams's brash personality didn't help matters. During his presidency he avoided social functions with no understanding of how insulting he appeared. Once he even refused an invitation to a ball to honor George Washington. Instead of attending, Adams scrawled *DECLINED* on the invitation. By the time of the election of 1800, Adams had made far more enemies than he realized. Still, he did have supporters, and the Federalists nominated him for re-election. The Democratic-Republicans nominated Thomas Jefferson as their presidential candidate.

The mudslinging started early, and it quickly became ugly. Federalists accused Jefferson of being godless and sinful. If Jefferson was elected, they warned, terror and murder would break out across the land, and the ground would be soaked with blood. Anti-France groups accused Jefferson of loving France more than the United States. He was called a coward for not fighting in the Revolutionary War. He was also labeled a dishonest businessman and accused of being sexually immoral.

Thomas Jefferson

Adams fared badly too. Newspapers accused him of being weak and unmanly. They threw every accusation they could think of at him. He was labeled a fool, a tyrant, and a criminal. Detractors claimed he and the Federalists loved the British monarchy more than the United States. One ridiculous story accused Adams of trying to marry off one of his sons to the daughter of King George III to gain power and unite the United States with Britain.

Adams's most dangerous enemy turned out to be Alexander Hamilton. Hamilton didn't like or trust his fellow Federalist. Behind the scenes, Hamilton furiously wrote letters and spoke to friends against Adams's re-election. He hated Adams so much that he published an essay that listed all of Adams's mistakes as president. This essay deeply damaged Adams's reputation, which was already shaky.

John Adams was one of the many politicians Hamilton targeted in his writing.

LETTER

FROM

ALEXANDER HAMILTON,

CONCERNING

THE PUBLIC CONDUCT AND CHARACTER

OF

JOHN ADAMS, Esq.

PRESIDENT OF THE UNITED STATES.

NEW-YORK:

Printed for JOHN LANG, *by* GEORGE F. HOPKINS.

1800.

[*Copy-right secured.*]

When the votes were counted, Adams came in third, while Jefferson and Aaron Burr tied for the win. Jefferson became the third president when the House of Representatives broke the tie. Adams, defeated and demoralized, returned to Massachusetts. He would be remembered as being part of one of the dirtiest U.S. presidential campaigns in history.

ALIEN AND SEDITION ACTS

All his adult life, Adams fought for the rights of others. As a lawyer, he defended criminals and argued for the rule of law. As a founding father, he helped shape the Declaration of Independence. He was proud of the fact that he helped form a nation of good laws and inalienable rights. But during his presidency he supported a set of dangerous laws that could have undone the ideals he had fought so hard to create.

The war between France and Great Britain consumed Adams's administration. Soon after his election, Adams sent diplomats to France. The French demanded a $250,000 bribe, plus a loan of up to $12 million, just to begin negotiations. Adams refused to be bribed. He immediately ordered the diplomats to come home.

When word spread about the bribe, people were outraged. The Federalists demanded Adams declare war on France. Adams sided with Jefferson and the Democratic-Republicans who didn't want war.

But Jefferson refused to work with Adams. He knew that Adams was unpopular and disliked by many people in his party. Jefferson didn't want to be seen as supporting Adams in any way. This decision made the president look foolish. Members of his own party accused him of being pro-French. People were afraid that French spies had infiltrated the United States. Things got so bad that Abigail feared for her husband's safety.

Amidst this turmoil, the mostly Federalist Congress passed a series of four laws called the Alien and Sedition Acts. They were supposed to protect the United States against outside influences. What they really did was destroy some of the rights Adams and the other founding fathers had put in the Declaration of Independence.

The Naturalization Act changed the time an immigrant had to wait to become a citizen. Previously, an immigrant had to wait five years. The new law increased that time to 14 years.

The Alien Friends Act gave the president the power to deport any foreigner he thought dangerous. The Alien Enemies Act allowed the president to deport any immigrant from a country at war with the United States.

But the worst law was the Sedition Act. It made it illegal to speak or write anything against the government. This clearly unconstitutional act was directly against the basic American ideals of free speech and freedom of the press. The Democratic-Republicans strongly attacked this law. They argued that it violated the First Amendment.

Amazingly, Adams's own party, the Federalists, argued in favor of the law. They said that of course everyone was free to say or print anything they wanted. This law didn't stop that. All the law did, they said, was punish people after they spoke or published ideas against the government.

Adams knew exactly what these laws did. He understood that they opposed the constitution. But he considered them essential for a country about to go to war. In later years he called them "war measures." He also feared that if he didn't sign the laws, people would riot in the streets. The Federalist majority in Congress would attack him mercilessly. His urge to keep peace won over his misgivings about the rightness of the laws. It ended up being one of the biggest mistakes of his presidency.

Immediately after the laws went into effect, Federalists pored over newspapers to find any negative writings. Between 1798 and 1801, 25 people were prosecuted under the Sedition Act. Most of them were editors of Democratic-Republican newspapers that had published negative stories about Adams and the Federalists. Many other newspapers toned down their stories to protect themselves.

These laws launched a furious debate in state legislatures about the real meaning of "freedom of speech" and "freedom of the press." Some politicians saw the laws as a relief from the lies and slanderous statements published against them. Others, such as James Madison, said they attacked the right of free communication. Fortunately, the laws weren't in effect for long. They expired in 1801, when Jefferson became president.

Before the election of 1800, newspaper editors and Democratic-Republicans around the country used these laws to attack Adams's patriotism and integrity. These attacks helped Jefferson defeat him for the presidency.

By the Prefident of the United States of America.

A Proclamation.

WHEREAS by an act of the Congrefs of the United States, paffed the ninth day of February laft, entitled, "An act further to fufpend the commercial intercourfe between the United States and France, and the dependencies thereof," it is provided, That at any time after the paffing of this act, it fhall be lawful for the Prefident of the United States, if he fhall deem it expedient and confiftent with the interefts of the United States, by his order, to remit and difcontinue for the time being, the reftraints and prohibitions by the faid act impofed, either with refpect to the French Republic, or to any ifland, port or place, belonging to the faid Republic, with which a commercial intercourfe may fafely be renewed; and alfo to revoke fuch order, whenever in his opinion the intereft of the United States fhall require: and he is authorifed to make proclamation thereof accordingly.

And whereas the arrangements which have been made at St. Domingo for the fafety of the commerce of the United States, and for the admiffion of American veffels into certain ports of that ifland, do in my opinion, render it expedient and for the intereft of the United States to renew a commercial intercourfe with fuch ports.

Therefore I JOHN ADAMS, *President of the United States*, by virtue of the powers vefted in me by the above recited act, do hereby remit and difcontinue the reftraints and prohibitions therein contained, within the limits and under the regulations here following, to wit:

1. It fhall be lawful for veffels which have departed or may depart from the United States, to enter the ports of Cape Francois, and Port Republicain, formerly called Port au Prince, in the faid ifland of St. Domingo, on and after the firft day of Auguft next.

2. No veffel fhall be cleared for any other port in St. Domingo, than Cape Francois and Port Republicain.

3. It fhall be lawful for veffels which fhall enter the faid ports of Cape Francois and Port Republicain, after the thirty-firft day of July next, to depart from thence to any other port in faid ifland between Monte Chrifti on the North, and Petit Goave on the Weft; provided it be done with the confent of the government of St. Domingo, and purfuant to certificates or paffports expreffing fuch confent, figned by the conful-general of the United States, or conful refiding at the port of departure.

4. All veffels failing in contravention of thefe regulations, will be out of the protection of the United States, and be moreover liable to capture, feizure, and confifcation.

(L. S.) Given under my hand and the feal of the United States, at Philadelphia, the twenty-fixth day of June, in the year of our Lord 1799, and of the Independence of the faid States, the twenty-third.

JOHN ADAMS.

By the President.
TIMOTHY PICKERING, Secretary of State.

Extract of a letter from ROBERT LISTON, ESQ. Minifter Plenipotentiary of his Britannic Majefty to the United States, dated New-York, July 13, 1799, to his Excellency Vice Admiral SIR HYDE PARKER.

"I Have juft learnt with concern, by a letter from Brigadier General Maitland, dated at Sea, (lat. 35, N. long. 68, W.) the 2d of this month, that there has been a mifunderftanding on the fubject of the time fixed for renewing the commercial intercourfe between the United States and St. Domingo.

"In the agreement entered into by General Maitland and myfelf with the American minifters, it was clearly underftood by all parties and fixed,—that *the stipulated ports in the island should be opened on a certain day* for the reception of the merchant veffels of Great Britain and the United States; NOT *that the ports of America and of Jamaica should be opened on a certain day*. In confequence of

CHAPTER FIVE

LASTING LEGACY

John Adams had spent most of his life alone, or feeling that way. As a young lawyer, he spent days traveling on lonely country roads. He was absent from his beloved Abigail and their farm for months and years at a time. He felt alone and unwanted during most of his time in Europe. As vice president, he was isolated from Washington and Congress. And as president, he chose to set himself apart from politics, trusting few and listening to no one but Abigail.

Some of his isolation was by choice. At other times, it was his rudeness, aloofness, and lack of social skills that pushed him to the edges of society. Part of his legacy is his isolation and inability to be part of the social life of the United States.

But Adams wasn't always alone. He was a part of a group of people who accomplished something remarkable.

They formed a new country from scratch. His real legacy was that he worked tirelessly and supported the revolution.

Adams never refused a call to serve. He was the one who stood up at the Second Continental Congress and said yes, we need an army, and George Washington should lead it. He sat on committees, debated ideas, edited the Declaration of Independence, and negotiated with foreign governments in the name of freedom. No other founding father worked as hard, traveled as far, or sacrificed as much of his personal life as Adams.

He was never afraid to stand up for what he believed in. He didn't care what anyone else thought as long as he was convinced it was the right thing to do. This quality was also his greatest downfall. His unwavering belief that he was always right cost him friends and allies. It made enemies and broke the hearts of his friends and family. But to him, it was all worth it in the end. He had helped to create a nation and lived to see it grow and thrive.

TIMELINE

1735

John Adams is born on October 19 in Braintree, Massachusetts.

1751

Adams is admitted to Harvard College at the age of 15.

1758

Adams becomes a lawyer.

1764

Adams marries Abigail Smith.

1770

The Boston Massacre occurs on March 5.
Adams defends the British soldiers at their trial.

1774

Adams is chosen as a delegate to the Continental Congress.

1775

The Battle of Lexington and Concord occurs on April 19.
Adams goes to Philadelphia for the Second Continental Congress.
He nominates George Washington to lead the Continental Army.

1776

Adams and the other delegates to the Second Continental Congress sign the Declaration of Independence on July 4.

1779

Adams writes the Massachusetts Constitution. He then returns to Europe to negotiate peace with the British.

1781

The Continental Army defeats British forces at Yorktown.
British troops there surrender.

1782

The Netherlands recognizes the United States as an independent nation.

1783

Adams, along with Benjamin Franklin and John Jay, sign the Treaty of Paris, which ends the Revolutionary War.

1785

Adams is appointed ambassador to Great Britain.

1789

Washington is elected president, and Adams is elected vice president.

1792

Washington and Adams are re-elected.

1796

Adams is elected second president of the United States, defeating Thomas Jefferson.

1798

Adams creates the U.S. Navy Department.

1800

Adams runs for re-election and loses to Thomas Jefferson.

1824

Adams's son John Quincy Adams is elected president of the United States.

1826

Adams dies at age 91 on July 4. Thomas Jefferson dies this same day.

GLOSSARY

ambassador—a government official who represents his or her country in a foreign country

anonymous—written, done, or given by a person whose name is not known or made public

courtier—an attendant at a royal court

delegate—a person who represents a larger group of people at a meeting

elector—one of a group of people who vote to choose between two or more people running for office

envoy—a diplomat

epoch—an important period in time

inauguration—the formal ceremony to swear a person into political office

massacre—the needless killing of a group of helpless people

merchant—a person who buys and sells goods for profit

monarch—someone who rules over a kingdom, such as a king

negotiate—to bargain or discuss something to come to an agreement

obstinate—stubborn

rebellion—a fight against the people in charge

sedition—actions or words meant to stir up rebellion against a government

slovenly—untidy or unclean in appearance

sovereign—having an independent government

FURTHER READING

Lassieur, Allison. *Building a New Nation: an Interactive American Revolution Adventure*. North Mankato, MN: Capstone Press, 2019.

Quirk, Anne. *The Good Fight: The Feuds of the Founding Fathers and How they Shaped the Nation*. New York: Alfred A. Knopf, 2017.

Roxburgh, Ellis. *Thomas Jefferson vs. John Adams: Founding Fathers and Political Rivals*. New York: Gareth Stevens Publishing, 2016.

Seeley, MH. *Before John Adams Was President*. New York: Gareth Stevens Publishing, 2018.

INTERNET SITES

America's Library
www.americaslibrary.gov/aa/adams/aa_adams_subj.html

National Park Service
www.nps.gov/adam/john-adams-biography.htm?&NMW_TRANS=ext

The Smithsonian
www.si.edu/spotlight/knowing-the-presidents-john-adams

The White House
www.whitehouse.gov/about-the-white-house/presidents/john-adams/

SOURCE NOTES

Page 6, "I am not..." David McCullough. *John Adams*. New York: Simon and Schuster, 2001, p. 42.

Page 7, "There are very few..." John Adams, "Letter from John Adams to Abigail Adams, 18 August 1776."

Page 14, "He can't dance..." Jonathan Sewall, "Letter from Jonathan Sewall to Judge Lee, September 21, 1787."

Page 15, "We worked in strange..." "John Jay and the Treaty of Paris," StudyLib, https://studylib.net/doc/8873268/john-jay-and-the-treaty-of-paris, Accessed April 15, 2019.

Page 19, "the most insignificant..." John Adams. *Letters of John Adams, Addressed to His Wife*. Boston. C.C. Little and J. Brown, 1841, p. 133.

Page 28, "one of the best pieces..." John Adams. *Diary and Autobiography of John Adams (1815)*. Cambridge, MA: The Belknap Press of Harvard University Press, 1961.

Page 29, "[Adams] is always..." Stacy Schiff, "Franklin in Paris," *The American Scholar,* March 1, 2009, theamericanscholar.org/franklin-in-paris/#.XIwMtC2ZMxd, Accessed March 15, 2019.

Page 30, "[Adams] hates Franklin..." Gordon Wood. *Revolutionary Characters: What Made the Founding Fathers Different*. New York: Penguin Press, 2006, p 177.

Page 32, "I can do..." John Adams, "Letter from John Adams to Abigail Adams, 16 July 1776."

Page 33, "If you do not..." "John Adams Was A Tiger Dad. So Was John Quincy." New England Historical Society, www.newenglandhistoricalsociety.com/john-adams-tiger-dad-john-quincy/, Accessed March 15, 2019.

Page 35, "cloud over my..." John R. Howe Jr., "John Adams's Views on Slavery," *The Journal of Negro History,* July 1964.

Page 40, "Reason first..." "Writing the Declaration of Independence, 1776," EyeWitness to History, www.eyewitnesstohistory.com/jefferson.htm, Accessed March 15, 2019.

Page 42, "before I reported..." "The Declaration of Independence: A History" National Archives, www.archives.gov/founding-docs/declaration-history, Accessed March 15, 2019.

Page 42, "will be the most..." *John Adams*, p. 130.

Page 44, "if this had been..." Sean Lawler, "John Adams, Diplomat to France," Boston Tea Party Ships and Museum, August 23, 2014, www.bostonteapartyship.com/john-adams-diplomat-france, Accessed March 15, 2019.

Page 45, "meet the friendship..." Peter Carlson, "Encounter: John Adams' Bow to King George III," HistoryNet, December, 2012, https://www.historynet.com/encounter-john-adams-bow-king-george-iii.htm, Accessed April 15, 2019.

SELECT BIBLIOGRAPHY

John Adams
whitehouse.gov/about-the-white-house/presidents/john-adams

John Adams Historical Society
john-adams-heritage.com

Massachusetts Government
mass.gov/guides/john-adams-the-massachusetts-constitution

McCullough, David. *John Adams*. New York: Simon and Schuster, 2001.

National Archives
archives.gov/founding-docs/more-perfect-union

Wood, Gordon. *Revolutionary Characters: What Made the Founders Different*. New York: Penguin Press, 2006.

INDEX